Remnants of Imagination Eroding Over Time

Abann Or

BookLeaf Publishing

Presentation by *BookLeaf Publishing*

Web: www.bookleafpub.com

E-mail: info@bookleafpub.com

ISBN: 9789357616843

First edition 2022

JVP

PREFACE

I think that even when my writings present as sad or dark or depressing they don't necessarily exist, for me, in that way. My brain is different. It processes things in a unique way and my emotions fire in a unique way. My writings celebrate something specific and special and private to me. They're not perfect, and I don't expect them to be, but they're mine.

Give and Take

The razors edge
Never cared to perceive of
Pain it afforded the flesh
That neither cared nor conceive of
The cutting and shaping
That sharpened
The razors edge

As a Delicacy

In the grip of time,
Death's rampant greed,
Suckles the milk of life,
Sups from the hand that feeds,
No intent to nourish the starved,
Only to tweak, to tease,
But to appease their hunger,
Or to feed their need?
Never these.
No, never these.

As the meal is finished,
Hear the chime of strings,
Drawn through Satan's teeth,
Used to floss his grin,
Each strand formed,
From angels wings,
Tools to the serve the wicked,
Plucked from innocent things,
Always this.
Yes, always this.

Controlled [Substance] Anarchy

I have emotionally
Defunct episodes, only
In a controlled [substance]
Sort of way.

Suffocated by
apathy's callous
grip 'round
My throat.

I won't topple into
Dark desolation today, only
In a controlled [substance]
Sort of delay.

Often I find myself
Testing my lean
Over the edge
Just a tiny bit further

Craving the familiar
All-consuming unwell of it, only
In a controlled [substance]
Sort of waning restraint.

Let me be
Free to drown
In the deep
Dark decay

I want to free fall
I want the plummet, only
In a controlled [substance]
Sort of abandonment.

Yet I hover
Paralyzed
Suspended
In place

Tablets prescribed deflate
Risky intentions, only
In a controlled [substance]
Sort of cliche.

Of Self and Soul

Does one measure the worth of a soul
By each bead of blood as it drops
Or is it weighed as a whole
Only as the beating heart stops
And does its worth change
From glass shards and steel nails
That have tattered and shredded
While imbedding the tales
Of woeful departures
Of memories long forgot
Or of those we should have buried
But simply did not
Does the good one invests
Add value to the whole
Only to have sins detract merit
By the pound from one's soul
In the end of it all
What point is there to this
If a soul not intended for purchase
Was meant as a presentable gift
Who to us did the giving
And to whom should we give
So that in the midst of our life
We know we truly did live

As Fodder for the Glutton

I swallowed too much shame today
And it lodged deep inside my throat
Humiliation tried to squeeze it out
But his grip ensured that I would choke
I thought to grease my gullet
With a nice big dose of pride
But with humiliations grip around my neck
Even pride couldn't slide inside
Disgrace happened by on purpose
To shake his bobble-head at me
And wagged his finger back and forth
To blame me for my own misery
So I sat there turning blue
Until patience walked up to us to see
And asked humiliation, pride, and disgrace
If they'd kindly let me be
Humiliation loosened up his grip
Grumbling as he stomped away
Disgrace and pride left in stride
Promising to return again someday
Patience fed grace to me like honey
And used forgiveness to pat my back
Before I knew, shame dropped into my gut
No different than any other snack

The Masquerade

Fake smile
Blank stare
Another sign
Of the facade I'm wearing
Porcelain
Cracked skin
Another sign
That it's crumbling
Colors fade
Outside in
Another sign
My pretense is waning
Weak breaths
Empty chest
Another sign
The mask is suffocating
Me.

Every Form of Change

Change in the pocket
can burn a hole inside,
wider than the swing
of a reapers scythe.

Change sounds its rattle
in a poor man's grip,
because two-cents-worth
means they've gone all in.

Change set loose
from the insolvents grip,
is what can reclaim a soul
that's been spread too thin.

Change hitting the table
means the price has been paid,
as a feast is to the starved
so is release for the enslaved.

Change fully rendered
supports dreaming big,
and change is the only
currency of better things.

Of The Forge

Rage of the breaths left wasted
Ripped from within my chest
Forced from the chains that anchor
The wrath of a broken mess
Bound to the heart that's weeping
Laid amongst the burning coal
Forged is the key to my heart
Pulled from my surging soul

By the Light

I'm pressing against
The in-between
Of nothing much
And everything
Can't cross over yet
But I see the green
On the other side
Of the splitting seam

Hard Logic

I remember
Mother inhaled,
The haar
Complied,
Rolling inward.

Feral echos
A free-range panic,
The waves
Subside,
The offing stagnates.

Refined, As Is

Sins that my father
Poured out
On my pyre
Reigned like an oil
Causing flames
To climb higher

Ashes got deepest
Where embers
Burned brighter
Inferno consuming
Spreading heat
Even wider

As all that I couldn't be
Piles up wood

As all that I wouldn't
Becomes sacrificed goods

As all that I was
Can never come back

As all that I wasn't
Sifts right through my hand

As all that I am
Falls short of all that it should

As all that I wanted
Starves for all that it could

As all that I hope for
Becomes all I might be

I am refined by the flames
Into all that is me

Grim is the Reaper

biting down too hard
on my tongue-in-cheek
severs what's left
unspoken between
gridlock teeth
savory salt of the
earthquake beneath
my feet, grim is the
reaper sewing seed
in my bundling sheet

Where We Go to Drown

Are we created to remain
On the in-between
Of all we will be
And all we've been?

Sight Unseen

What eyes perceive as changing patterns
Fingers read like scattered scars
Eyes trace along uneven edges
Though fingertips don't reach that far
As they race across the clouds
Cast wide as a fishing net
Jumping through each square
Like hopscotch overtop the fence
Sliding through the sand dunes
To climb a rocky ledge
Getting caught up in the gusting winds
Humming a silent cacophony of tunes
Reminding our eyes to search for more
Than a pretty place to land
Because to truly see the entire world
We should feel every detailed strand

Higher Power

Father bears his responsibility like a song. Like a melody of grandeur. He, the climax of a poem that won't ever rhyme but goes on and on long after the music has begun its gentle fade from our ears. And similar to a beatboxer, the powerful swelling and surging of sounds materialize as a mirage. We look around him, and below him, and above him, for sign of a recording device to dispel the illusion captivating us when, eventually with certainty, we find an area to dwell in the comfort of a reality where we know without question that the living breathing vibrations always resonate from deep within his being. There's no trickery here where He swaddles us in the universe and wraps forever around us encouraging us to paint it with every color waiting just below the surface of our soul. Here where He has centered a whole planet at the core of all that we are, allowing us to decorate it as he guides it in how to decorate us too, not as we would a blank canvas but as we would when aspiring to layer beauty over top of beauty until we are the culmination of the masterpieces we were created to be.

Manifesting as a Love Letter

My Dearest,

I remember you.
How beautiful.
How Precious.
How unique.

How as a child you curled up in my arms and let me twist your hair as I hummed with the tune of sorrow and loneliness aching in your heart. You sighed as I braided darkness around each strand. You surrendered the exhale of innocence against the strength of my embrace, and when you breathed in deep the air from your lungs I first knew life.

I remember you.
How small.
How delicate.
How fragile.

How as you grew you opened the door wide to me night after night as in sleep you caved to the madness unleashed within your mind. You wept as I crawled inside and painted pictures ever more vibrant and vivid and real. You surrendered the recognition of peace against the backdrop of my artistic creation, and when I drank deep the tears from your eyes I knew fulfillment.

I know you.
How frantic.
How desperate.
How lost.

How you falter as you feel my shadow churn and test the inner confines of your flesh. You bleed as I dig in deep to carve a home where I can reach and stretch and grow. You surrender the remembrance of calm against the swell of pitch black, and as I am embraced deep within the hollow of your soul I know love.

I remember you. I know you. You are my breath of life, my everlasting fulfillment, my one true love.

I am not sure how long I will be away but I will return as soon as I am able.

Warmest wishes until I return,

Darkness

Where the Wild is

the world
rests on
our shoulders
like a
razor blade
slicing open
a weightless
darkness rages
silence falling
dripping dropping
circling down
the drain
with wild
intentions
as it's
only vengeance
It whispers:
"Won't you come and play?"

Truth Found in Every Wishing Well

There was a ruler of unimaginable wealth who, despite his riches, deemed his prized possession to be the vast sinkhole located in the center of his empire. A chasm that, he boasted, had no end.

Only a beginning.

He gloated about owning the Beginning, and that just like it, he too would have no end.

Those the ruler welcomed onto his estate as his guest grew tired of the constant bragging. They would pit their own wealth against that of the rulers. If they should find the end, the ruler would forfeit everything to them, but if they did not, they would forfeit all their earthly possessions to him.

Inevitably the ruler won, and because he possessed more than he could fathom, he would force the losers to watch him cast every bit of their worldly wealth down onto the endless void. They were forced to stand and listen as their life's legacy disappeared without a sound into the black abyss. Then he'd force them to strip naked and even the clothes off their back was fed to the Beginning.

"I wish you well," The ruler bellowed at them as they retreated, shame and desolation gnashing at their bare heels.

Little by little, visitors stopped coming to his estate. The ruler was forced to sit by himself, staring into the darkness, wondering of its vastness. Several years passed without a single challenger and the ruler convinced himself that, apart from his own estate, he must have cleared the entire world of all possessions.

The ruler would stare down into the cavernous void and try to recall all he had thrown down into it. As the years continued to roll by, he remembered less and less of the specifics of these things until a new obsession began to take root.

Sure, he owned the Beginning, but possession of at least one thing that had eluded him this entire time - the End.

It started out small. With mere trinkets. He cast them down into the depths one by one as he watched and listened intently for a sign of the End he was seeking. When this proved futile the ruler ordered more to be thrown down into the cavern. He enlisted help from subjects and servants alike, to bring in endless succession, possession after possession to feed Beginning's insatiable hunger for more.

Day and night they toiled in vain until early one morning there was a breakthrough.

A weary old man, carrying too heavy an object, walked too close to the edge and slipped down into the hole. At first the shock of this misstep held the old man's voice, and as the ruler watched him disappear into the midst of the obsidian core, there was no sound. It seemed forever had passed when a great surging of black bubbled up from the confines of the earths core. The darkness swelled up over the edges before popping as if pricked with the sharp edge of an invisible sewing needle. A faint - nearly inaudible - sound emerged like a puff of air, and the ruler was certain it was the dying echo of a terrified scream.

"I wish you well." The ruler murmured sanctimoniously.

The wave of darkness settled back down as if not remembering having had a voice for the first time.

The ruler hid, waiting for the next unsuspecting servant carrying the next load of possessions. This time he crept up and shoved. The shriek of horror came immediately and the ruler mused as the sound was not consumed by the darkness, but instead rode it as if the two became one entity. Eventually the sound died out, but after a while of watching and waiting, a bubbling up of black shadow broke free from the confines of the cavern once again.

"I wish you well."

The ruler made up his mind in that moment. If it was impossible to go down into the depths to take possession of the End, he would fill the void and bring the End to the Beginning.

Efforts were doubled, then tripled, allowing no respite from the obsession driving the ruler to spill down into the chasm everything in pursuit of the End. When his material possessions began to dwindle the ruler dragged subject and servant alike into the open mouth of the Beginning.

"I wish you well."

Early one morning, as the ruler stood perplexed overlooking the Beginning - overlooking his great Wishing Well - he felt a tiny hand at the small of his back. Turning his head, he saw a boy.

"You see, my boy, what all of this 'wishing well' has done for me? I am no closer to the End than I am here, at the very Beginning. I have given everything I possess to achieve what I seek most in this life and for what?"

"You haven't given everything, master."

The ruler looked at the boy with hope and expectation that some hidden alcove of goods had been discovered for use as an offering. "Tell me, boy, and tell me quick, what more do I have to give?"

"Yourself."

The hand on the rulers back turned rigid, and as he slipped over the edge into the darkness, he was able to find his voice.

“I wish you well.” Said the boy as he sat at the edge, dreaming and scheming of the untold riches existing at the bottom of the cavern. He began planning and plotting just how he might retrieve it from the depths of the Wishing Well to possess all the riches for himself.

www.ingramcontent.com/pod-product-compliance
Lightning Source LLC
Chambersburg PA
CBHW062205160726
48282CB00027B/1003
* 9 7 8 9 3 5 7 6 1 6 8 4 3 *